SACRAMENT SERIES

MARRIAGE

Cardinal Jorge Medina Estévez
Foreword by Cardinal Julián Herranz

Libreria Editrice Vaticana

United States Conference of Catholic Bishops
Washington, DC

Translation of *Sei sposato o pensi di sposarti?*

Cover © Masterfile.

Scripture excerpts used in this work are taken from the *New American Bible, revised edition* © 2010, 1991, 1986, 1970 Confraternity of Christian Doctrine, Inc., Washington, DC. All rights reserved. No part of this work may be reproduced or transmitted in any form or by any means, electronic or mechanical, including photocopying, recording, or by any information storage and retrieval system, without permission in writing from the copyright owner.

Excerpts from the *Catechism of the Catholic Church*, second edition, copyright © 2000, Libreria Editrice Vaticana–United States Conference of Catholic Bishops, Washington, DC. Used with permission. All rights reserved.

English translation copyright © 2014, Libreria Editrice Vaticana (LEV), Vatican City State. All rights reserved.

First printing, February 2015

ISBN 978-1-60137-447-9

TABLE OF CONTENTS

FOREWORD	1
INTRODUCTION	3
A LOOK AT THE PRESENT SITUATION	5
THE CHRISTIAN VIEW OF MARRIAGE	9
ADVANCE PREPARATION FOR MARRIAGE	17
CHOICE OF A FUTURE SPOUSE	19
PROXIMATE PREPARATION FOR MARRIAGE	25
CELEBRATION OF MARRIAGE	27
THE CHRISTIAN FAMILY AND HOME CONSTITUTE A DOMESTIC CHURCH	29
SEPARATION, DIVORCE, NULLITY OF MARRIAGE	33
CONCLUSION	37

FOREWORD

In the Year of Faith announced by our Holy Father Benedict XVI, we are called to "stronger ecclesial commitment to new evangelization in order to rediscover the joy of believing and the enthusiasm for communicating the faith" (Pope Benedict XVI, Motu Proprio *Porta Fidei*, no. 7).

I can say that this invaluable pamphlet follows precisely the direction indicated by the Pope, because my dear friend, Cardinal Jorge Medina, has written these pages with the expertise, passion, and apostolic zeal of a believer who is making every effort to communicate the faith with the immediacy and clarity required by our particular cultural context. The author has masterfully drawn on his long experience as theologian, member of the International Theological Commission and the Committee for the Drafting of the *Catechism of the Catholic Church*; as pastor, ever attentive to the needs of the People of God; and as teacher, eager to instruct the faithful in the central truths of Christian doctrine, keeping in mind individual and social circumstances.

It seems to me that this useful catechetical tool is addressed to all believers, to lead them to a thorough assimilation of the theology of the Sacrament of Matrimony, with the sense of responsibility of one who is called to "give an explanation to anyone who asks you for a reason for your hope" (1 Pt 3:15). But it is addressed in a special way to those who are about to embark on the path to holiness in married life, as well as to the priests who prepare engaged couples to receive this sacrament.

The new evangelization necessarily passes through the shining witness of Christian families. Indeed, in opening the Synod of Bishops, Benedict XVI said: "Matrimony is a Gospel in itself, a Good News for the world of today." Therefore, I sincerely hope that this book will be used to rediscover the full value of the Sacrament of Matrimony with which God himself seals the mutual gift of man and woman, perfects their love, strengthens their indissoluble unity and helps them to attain holiness in married life, generously welcoming the children the Lord may wish to give them and raising them as true children of God.

Cardinal Julián Herranz
President Emeritus
Pontifical Council for Legislative Texts

INTRODUCTION

Are you planning to get married? Are you married? In either case, there will be people around you who are married or who intend to get married soon. In all probability, you came into the world in the bosom of a family built on the foundation of marriage. Perhaps you have thought about this reality and have seen painful situations where a marriage was unhappy or even failed. Or, perhaps you have had contact with widowers or widows who, after a more or less long married life, have suffered the loss of a spouse and may live in painful solitude.

A LOOK AT THE PRESENT SITUATION

To look at a situation objectively is an exercise in wisdom, while to ignore it is foolishness.

The present situation of marriage, largely in the Western world, is cause for very grave concern for us who are blessed by the fact that we are Catholic and reflect our beliefs in the Word of God, read in the rich tradition of the Church and as proposed by the Magisterium of its lawful pastors. We have received from the Lord Jesus the task of keeping, defending, and spreading the truth of the Gospel that leads us to true freedom (Cf. Jn 8:32).

Since ancient times, the institution of marriage has been threatened by the scourge of divorce, often accepted in civil law. The ease with which some civil laws authorize the dissolution of a marriage becomes a reason for spouses not to worry about the difficulties, at times serious, that they can experience in their life together, even at the cost of great sacrifices. Thus they find it easy to regard divorce as a legitimate way to "rebuild their lives" and enter into a new union. And society, profoundly secularized and de-Christianized, accepts these new unions as if they were legitimate and worthy of consideration and respect. The terrible consequences of divorce generally have more serious effects on women and children. Divorce followed by a civil union constitutes *adultery*. Given that this state is a grave and permanent sin, the view of the Church is that people who find themselves in such a situation cannot receive Holy Communion. This is not because of a prohibition of the Church that she herself could change but rather because living in serious sin is a contradiction to receiving the Body of Christ, which implies accepting and fulfilling the law of God (Cf. 1 Cor 11:28).

Unfortunately it often happens that, even though they do not get to the point of separation or divorce, some people united by the marriage bond have sexual relations, casual or habitual, with another person who is single, or even worse, married. These situations, considered illegal in the past, are largely equated with civil unions in many nations: the end result is that marital infidelity is minimized. The icing on the cake is the view, obviously sexist, that betrayals by wives are considered worse than those by husbands. In the Christian vocabulary, this type of union constitutes an act of *adultery*.

In recent years, more and more often we find cases of people who are able to contract marriage but do not do so and are content to live as if they were already married, without the nuptial bond. Sometimes these people intend to get married later, in time, but in many cases they are satisfied with living together. There are civil laws that grant legal, economic, health, and social benefits in general, even to these unions, so that they are recognized practically as substitutes for married life. In this way these civil laws depreciate marriage; they allow the union between man and woman to be separated from the natural responsibilities that flow from the complementarity between them and toward their children. Speaking as Christians—let us be clear—these situations represent a state of *concubinage* and a life in the permanent sin of *fornication*.

Throughout human history there has always been the practice of homosexuality, that is, sexual relations between persons of the same sex. Recently, these relationships have been defended, especially by groups who engage in them, as something normal, to be respected and provided with social and legal benefits. Homosexual pride is defended as an authentic value. The subject is complicated, since science has not yet found satisfactory answers concerning the origin of homosexuality. In any case, it is necessary to keep in mind the difference between the tendency and the practice of homosexuality. While there is no question that there is no guilt in the case of the first (although it is still considered a deformity), the *activity* is objectively and morally reprehensible and sinful. Some laws have granted legal privileges that support and protect people in homosexual relationships. Homosexual activity between men is called *sodomy*, and if practiced between women it is called *lesbianism*.

From a Christian perspective, and also from the viewpoint of the natural law, *adultery*, *fornication*, *concubinage*, and *lesbian* or *sodomitic* activity are immoral acts and therefore harmful for those who practice them and also to society.

The situation, then, is cause for concern, and a Catholic cannot be content to take note of the facts and remain indifferent. The future of the Church and the entire society depends to a large extent on marriage and the family. We are facing a challenge, and everyone must make a contribution if things are to change. The challenge begins by knowing the truth about marriage. Having taken this step, an examination of conscience will be required, and then with God's help we will need to roll up our sleeves in order to correct what needs to be corrected.

THE CHRISTIAN VIEW OF MARRIAGE

The Catholic teaching on marriage is presented in the *Catechism of the Catholic Church*, numbers 1601-1666, and in the *Compendium*, numbers 337-350.

Marriage has a human, biological, psychological, and social basis that goes far beyond the phenomenon of relationships between the sexes in the world of living things. Viewed from a faith perspective, the biological difference between man and woman acquires a deep spiritual meaning, which does not exclude the material but raises it to a higher and unexpected level.

Marriage is a human and Christian reality in which the contracting parties recognize and carry out a *vocation* or *call* from God, the mission entrusted by him in this world. It is a Christian response to a plan coming from God. It is an honor, a responsibility, a source of joy. Because the call comes from God himself, it brings with it the grace and divine help to live it fully, since it is a path to that holiness to which all Christians are called and in which the deepest and truest joy is found.

Christian marriage is built under the sign of *love*. To love is to give and be given. Love is the opposite of selfishness. It means to share, to forgive, and to serve rather than make the other person into one's servant. To love means to give up even things that are pleasant, when it is a question of seeking the other's good. To love means to take the initiative, to forget oneself, to learn gratitude and not become a mercenary; it means to be patient and understanding, to treat the other as one would wish to be treated. It is good to ask, do I have the right idea of what love is? Have I learned yet how to love? Do I recognize that I have not always known how to love?

The perfect *model* of love is God. He not only *has* love, he *is* love. That is what the Apostle John says (Cf. 1 Jn 4:16). God cannot stop loving, and all that he does, he does out of love. He loves freely: he has no need of anything to be happy, and the purpose of his creation is to communicate to his creatures something of his infinite goodness and complete happiness. God's love is a gift. Everything he has created is a gift, a donation, an act of unlimited generosity. "God so loved the world that he gave his only Son, so that everyone who believes in him may have eternal life" (Cf. Jn 3:16). Truly, the Father could give us no greater gift than his own Son, Jesus Christ. And I, have I loved him generously? Have I been able to give and, especially, to give myself? Have I been able to discover whether perhaps there are hidden traces of selfishness in my love? Do I try to purify my love?

God's love is *nuptial*. In the Old Testament, God presents himself as the bridegroom of his people (Cf. Hos 2; Ez 16; Sg). He is the bridegroom who anticipates himself in love, who loves mercifully, who showers his beloved bride with the greatest gifts, who endures betrayal, who forgives his unfaithful bride and lovingly welcomes her when she returns to him penitent.

In the New Testament, Jesus is the bridegroom of the Church (Cf. for example Mt 9:15, Lk 5:35, Eph 5:21-33, Rev 21:1 ff.). Just as the first woman, Eve, was formed from the rib of Adam while he was asleep (Cf. Gn 2:18-24), so also the Church was born on Calvary, when the Roman soldier pierced the side of Jesus with his lance, and from the wounded and lifeless heart of the Savior flowed blood and water (Cf. Jn 19:34), symbols of the Sacraments of Baptism and the Eucharist. God's nuptial love for the people of Israel and that of Jesus for his Church are the profound realities Christian marriage is called upon to reflect. I wonder how often it happens that those who wish to get married ask themselves whether they love their future spouse as Jesus loves his Church. And those who are already married, do they regard or at least try to regard their spouse as Christ regards his Church? This is not a romantic or idealistic view but rather what Christian married love must truly be.

Christian marriage is a *sacrament*. This means that it begins with a liturgical and symbolic rite, which derives effectiveness from its institution by Christ and from the action of the Holy Spirit, and which confers God's grace on those who receive it with the proper dispositions. Grace is a supernatural gift that makes a person like God, in his image. It may be compared to a garment that adorns its wearer and makes that person more beautiful or to an adoption that introduces a child into an adoptive family with the same rights as natural children. These comparisons are not perfect, since our human words are imperfect in conveying divine realities. Sacred Scripture teaches us that God is truly our Father (see Mt 5:45, 48; 6:4, 9, 15; 25:34; Jn 1:12; 2 Cor 6:18) and that we are truly his children (Cf. 1 Jn 3:1 ff.), provided, of course, that we live according to the Gospel. Although the celebration of the Rite of Marriage is brief, its spiritual effects are long-lasting, and the grace it communicates is meant to accompany spouses throughout their lives. It is like a solar battery: every time it comes into contact with the light, it generates energy.

God's *grace* is his gift that leads us to *holiness*, which is the vocation of every Christian. Holiness does not consist of acts or spectacular moments, but of faithfulness, day after day, to the will of God. Every Christian is called by Baptism to be *holy*, that is, to live for God (Cf. Rom 14:8), to love him above all things with our whole heart (Cf. Dt 6:5, Mt 22:37, Mk 12:30, Lk 10:27), and to love people and all of creation out of love for God and in the way he himself loves them. It is a big mistake to think that only priests and religious are called to holiness, as if other Christians could be satisfied with a life of mediocrity. But it is clear that the path by which each individual seeks holiness is different and depends on the situation in which God's providence has placed him or her.

For the vast majority of Christians, the path to holiness lies in marriage, professional responsibilities, daily work, and the other activities that make up their ordinary lives. For the Church's ministers, the pursuit of holiness takes place through the exercise of their ministry: proclamation of the Word of God, celebration of the sacraments, and pastoral service to the people. Religious, following their vocation, seek to respond to the call to holiness in fraternal community life and in the practice of the evangelical counsels, expressed in the vows of poverty, chastity, celibacy, and obedience to their superiors.

In her list of saints and blessed, the Church has placed the names of Christians who have lived in the most varied states of life: martyrs, bishops, priests, deacons, children, youth, adults, elderly, learned, farmers, rulers, people of high social rank, laborers, professionals, artists, etc. Many of these men and women lived in the married state. Certainly there are also other saints and blessed in heaven, but their holiness was known to God alone.

In their pursuit of holiness, married Catholics receive powerful help from the grace that comes from the Sacraments of Baptism, Confirmation, and Matrimony.

Naturally, marriage involves many temporal and material responsibilities, and these responsibilities are part of the spouses' Christian identity. But we must keep in mind that the efforts of Christian spouses cannot be limited to the attainment of material, social, educational, and physical well-being. The goal of their Christian vocation is above all to make spiritual progress in their life and to attain eternal happiness after the days of their earthly pilgrimage. For this reason, the environment of a Christian home must also necessarily include forms of prayer, participation in Sunday Mass, common reading of Sacred Scripture, and observance of the Church's prescribed penitential practices.

The spouses' love is *faithful*. In the Old Testament, God complained bitterly on various occasions when the people of Israel yielded to the temptation of idolatry, abandoning worship of the one true God to serve the false gods of the neighboring people. That sin of Israel was classified by the prophets as adultery, that is, as unfaithfulness to the nuptial covenant between God and Israel. Marital fidelity is thus a reflection of God's permanent and boundless love for his people and Christ's for his Church. Jesus established marital fidelity clearly and without exception, describing its transgression as *adultery* (Cf. Mt 5:32, Mk 10:11). Marital fidelity is a duty that obliges the husband as well as the wife all their lives; if one of the two dies, the living member can legitimately get married again to another person who is free to do so. Although the spouses' mutual fidelity is a legal bond (which must be observed as a matter of obligation), it is something deeper: it is also an expression of faithful love, exclusive and lifelong, of love in God, of tender, patient, suffering, and generous love. Faithfulness must be nurtured; spouses must avoid the occasions, dangerous friendships, or words that could damage it.

Love between the spouses must be open to *fruitfulness*, that is, to cooperation with God so that new children might come into this world. Fatherhood and motherhood are an echo of the astonishing fruitfulness that exists within God, One and Three, where from all eternity the Father begets his Son in the bond of love that is the Holy Spirit. Fruitfulness is an excellent form of giving. It is the handing over of one's own self, which is not limited to a single moment, but in fact becomes an almost indefinite series of acts of giving, caring, and striving, as well as sacrificing. Just as the relationship between the spouses springs from love and is called to perfection and to grow throughout their married life, so also fatherhood and motherhood are the school for a love that is called to grow. Children are always a blessing from God. At the same time they constitute, on God's part, an act of trust that the parents will gradually lead their children to assume their own responsibilities in this life without losing sight of the final goal, eternal happiness in the Kingdom of Heaven. No son or daughter is superfluous. All have the right to the love of a father and mother. The truth of Jesus' words, "It is more blessed to give than to receive" (Acts 20:35), is manifested in the responsibilities and love of the parents.

The spouses must responsibly and generously consider the number of children they are able to have, having recourse, if necessary, to natural methods for regulating births. But once conceived, a child's life is sacred and therefore must not lack for care, much less be attacked. To willingly cause an abortion is, according to the Second Vatican Council, an *abominable crime*, and the Church punishes it with the severe penalty of excommunication *latae sententiae*, that is, automatic. This punishment also falls on those who actively take part in the murder of the defenseless child, who is alive and in a mother's womb. The ultimate goal is for the child to become a son or daughter of God here on earth, as well as an heir to eternal life.

In married life, as in the life of every Christian, there are different kinds of *sufferings*: the death of dear ones, especially that of a spouse; various illnesses; misfortunes; undeserved animosities; family quarrels; moments of misunderstanding between spouses; a child who goes astray; failed projects, etc. In one way or another, every disciple of Jesus must take up the cross daily and follow him (Cf. Lk 9:23), knowing that the cross is a means of salvation, purification, and love. In moments of sorrow, spouses are called to sustain one another, to offer each other support, and to discover the message of love that the Lord's Cross is always there to be carried. Sufferings help us remember that this life is not the end and that complete happiness will be attained only in eternity.

ADVANCE PREPARATION FOR MARRIAGE

No important work can be completed overnight, just as no building can be reasonably constructed without first laying a foundation that is solid and sufficiently deep. Otherwise, at the least seismic movement, there is risk of seeing the poorly constructed building seriously fail or perhaps even collapse.

The foundation of a successful marriage is the Christian life of those who enter into it. A Christian life steeped in Christ; enlightened by his word, which is the word of truth; nourished by the sacraments of Baptism, Confirmation, the Eucharist, and Reconciliation. A life that is a constant practice of the Christian virtues of faith, hope, and charity, and the moral virtues of justice, fortitude, prudence, and temperance. A life in which there is enough time to pray, humbly asking God for the grace that our desires might be in accord with his holy will. A Christian life that has proved its consistency and authenticity in one's family and work, in responsibly fulfilling the obligations that arise from one's activities in this world, and in relating to others, inspired by the golden rule handed on by the Lord Jesus, when he urged us to treat other people the same as we would like to be treated by our fellow human beings (Cf. Mt 7:12).

Even if the engagement phase has not yet begun, every moment in the life of those who will later find their vocation in the married state is a little grain of sand or a little "brick," which serves to prepare, even without their knowing it, for a possible future marriage.

CHOICE OF A FUTURE SPOUSE

The choice of the man or woman who will be one's companion for life is a matter of utmost importance. To make it frivolously, by dwelling above all on secondary and irrelevant aspects, is extremely unwise and can cost very dearly.

The *physical aspect*, which is undeniably important because of the natural attraction it inspires, cannot be the only reason for one's choice: "All that glitters is not gold" and "appearances are deceiving." It is important to keep in mind that physical beauty is fleeting, while spiritual qualities are stable and enduring.

Material *wealth* should never be the chief reason for one's choice of a spouse. To look only at the worldly goods a person could bring in the form of a dowry or at one's desire for social and economic well-being radically alters the nature of love, as though it were a thing that could be purchased with money.

One who sees the future spouse as an object to satisfy one's sensuality sees the spouse as a thing and not as a person. Such a person reduces the spouse to the level of something pleasant to use and does not treat the spouse as someone to whom one gives oneself and whom one loves generously and unselfishly.

Taking a reasonable amount of time to get to know each other will certainly help a man and woman determine whether the future spouse possesses the desirable qualities to form a stable, fulfilling, and enduring family life.

In all likelihood, not all of the best and most desirable qualities may be found in the partner, but there are a few that seem especially important and should be carefully confirmed.

First of all, *sincerity*. An untruthful person who has a habit of lying, especially in important matters, does not inspire confidence, an essential part of love. Without trust and honesty, what one builds is built, as it were, on sand.

Next, *generosity*. The ability to give and to surrender is an expression of true love. Conversely, *selfishness* is a poison that corrodes love. Only one who believes that "it is better to give than to receive" (Acts 20:35) is prepared to love sincerely.

Finally, *industriousness*. A love for work, overcoming laziness, and striving to carry out one's responsibilities fully and effectively. These human qualities make us appreciate the people who possess them. They engender esteem and respect and strengthen the bonds between the individuals. After marriage, industriousness is essential for the well-being of the family, but it must be combined with the necessary commitment to live at home, with spouse and children, in such a way that work responsibilities do not interfere with domestic life.

What's more, spouses should respect the same *values* and *principles*. Marital sharing is by nature very deep. Were it based only on the external and material appearances of well-being, a marriage would be very superficial and even frivolous. On a human level, values and principles give people true dignity. Beyond the natural level, religious faith plays an important role in marital sharing. If the spouses share the same Christian and Catholic faith, that element will contribute powerfully to unity and will be important in moments of difficulty or crisis. One difficulty, certainly, is the absence of a shared religious faith, which creates areas of noncommunication that are hard to deal with successfully and are inevitably painful. Any Catholic who intends to marry someone who is not must reflect seriously on the implications of this situation. If the other party is a Christian, there will be a certain common ground, even if not as broad as would be desirable. If the other person is not a Christian or is an agnostic or atheist, the problems will be greater. And experience shows that when one of the spouses is a Muslim, this difference is almost impossible to overcome and inevitably leads to insoluble crises.

Attention must be paid to the future spouse's *character*. People who are violent or rigid by nature, who are stubborn and tend to hold grudges, usually cause frequent misunderstandings in a marriage. People who are pushy and overbearing, selfish and proud, offer little chance for a healthy and well-balanced married life. The psychology of the future spouse's personality is very important, especially if it is on the border between what is considered "normal" and what is abnormal.

It is also important to know if one's future spouse *loves his or her family*: parents, grandparents, brothers, and sisters. A deep love for one's family is a major factor in providing stability and balance. In married life, each spouse must have respect and love for the other's relatives, unless there are clear moral reasons that would justify distancing oneself. Love for the other spouse's family must be joined with due respect for the privacy and intimacy of their own home, which can be jeopardized by a relative's unwise meddling or intrusion, even if well intentioned.

Last, but certainly not least, it is important to mention the *ability to recognize one's mistakes*. It is a form of sincerity and love for the truth and an exercise of the virtue of humility, so important in every type of human relationship. People who admit mistakes do not become less valuable or weaker; rather they realize that they are limited creatures, in need of forgiveness even as they must always be ready to forgive. Admitting mistakes is generally a useful way to gain the right to forgiveness and reconciliation and a remedy for harmful feelings of resentment.

Sometimes an affectionate friendship or, later, an engagement carried on without due chastity, leaves the future wife pregnant. Even though marriage is a proper way to assume responsibility for the child yet to be born, nevertheless the man and woman have no moral obligation to get married if there is no true love and the other conditions that guarantee, as far as humanly possible, a happy marriage. Marriage must never be simply a way to "fix" a child's birth certificate.

Everything that has been said above is a call for reflection to not act hastily, to examine one's conscience, and exercise reasonable self-criticism, accompanied, of course, by prayer that the Lord may give the necessary grace to seek always and above all his holy will.

Although it may seem unpopular, it is impossible to slip past silently the subject of *premarital sexual relations*. Here we are not speaking of just any kind of lust but specifically of intimate relations between persons who intend to marry within a more or less short period of time. In modern language, these relations are called "proofs of love." But are they really? It is not a question here of denying that those who engage in premarital sexual relations sincerely love each other but of analyzing whether these expressions correspond to what in the Christian view deserves to be called true *love*.

The emotional relationship between the engaged couple cannot, of course, be equated with that which exists between husband and wife. Those who have assumed the marriage bond have *really* taken one another and have accepted, for their entire lives, mutual responsibilities and shared sacrifices and common burdens; and they are open to welcoming the children that will be the natural fruit of their spiritual and bodily union. This does not yet exist among the engaged. They have not assumed mutual responsibilities, and in most cases they try to avoid physical contact and its natural result.

Sexual relations are characterized as being a *symbol*. They are a reality that expresses the totality of mutual gifts and responsibilities, which will *really* exist only in marriage. Apart from marriage, or prior to marriage, sexual relations are like a symbol that lacks real content, a sign without meaning, or as one might say in the language of business, a check without funds, a piece of paper that is supposed to correspond to existing assets that in reality do not yet exist. It is a falsehood and a lie. Many engaged couples have probably never reflected on the non-truth of premarital relations and maintain the reassuring but false idea that they are acts of love. In fact, they are not acts of love, but rather displays of selfishness and the pursuit of pleasure without assuming the burden of sacrifice, by no means small, involved in the married state. They are disordered acts, because they take place outside the context God has willed for them, and for this reason, they are sinful. And sin is what alienates us from God and thus hurts us. In the case of premarital relations, those who allow themselves to be led to expressions of pleasure hurt themselves, perhaps without being fully aware of it. That which hurts the beloved cannot be called true love. To prevent this from happening, it is necessary to pray and to curb expressions of affection that might lead to excitement, to avoid situations that would severely test the persons' frailty and concupiscence. These are the wounds and scars of original sin. Well-balanced self-control is called *chastity*, a beautiful virtue that limits disorder and, in matters of sexuality, requires of Christians an ongoing and ennobling struggle that makes authentic love possible.

PROXIMATE PREPARATION FOR MARRIAGE

After the couple has spent a reasonable amount of time getting to know each other, the moment arrives to prepare for the celebration of marriage.

In the customs of some peoples, the intention to marry is expressed in a simple ceremony in which the engagement is formalized and the future spouses exchange engagement rings. In the Catholic Church, this exchange has a special seriousness and a religious meaning, expressed in the celebration of the liturgical rite of the blessing of the engagement rings, an official and public symbol of the engagement.

No doubt, there are many material needs that must be taken care of before the marriage celebration: preparing the future place of residence, choosing the church and its decorations, planning the lunch or dinner for the occasion, selecting clothing, etc. But this attention should not distract from what is most important: the religious and spiritual meaning of the married state. The marriage celebration should preferably be simple, not overly expensive or leave one with a huge debt. Above all, the celebration of the sacrament should not be postponed due to lack of funds for a lavish reception.

Two or three months before the wedding, the future spouses must go to the parish office where the bride has her domicile. There, the contracting parties will make the declarations required by church law and verify their true intent to consent to the marriage, as well as their freedom in view of the sacramental bond. These declarations are necessary so that the pastor, or the priest or deacon authorized by him, may proceed to the celebration of the Rite of Marriage.

In many dioceses, the bishops have determined that the future spouses must take part in marriage preparation conferences or encounters. These conferences are not a form of bureaucratic red tape but rather an aid to deepen a couple's awareness of the great importance of entering into the married *state*, as well as the natural and spiritual requirements that flow from this.

Future spouses need to be aware that the most important preparation is *spiritual*. Since marriage is a sacrament that confers the grace of God, it must be received with the proper disposition. During the engagement period, the future spouses should pray together and participate in Mass. They should discuss not only the material challenges of their future married life but also their responsibilities before God and how they will mutually support each other to grow in the Christian life. They must prepare themselves well to enter the married state; it is not only a civil and legal state, but also a state in the Church. Marriage is a particular Christian form of living out their pilgrimage to eternal life by loving each other in Christ, by producing new children of God, and by assuming the temporal responsibilities of the laity in various occupations.

CELEBRATION OF MARRIAGE

Before the marriage celebration, it is fitting and in fact may even be necessary for the future spouses to see a priest of their choice, go to confession, and receive absolution, forgiveness of their sins, and God's grace, which will be increased with the grace of the Sacrament of Marriage that will go with them all their lives. The wedding day should not be just concerned with the dress, the photos, the dinner, and the social obligations. It should be a time for recollection and prayer, so that the couple might enter the sanctuary of a new way of life—that of the *domestic Church*, filled with the presence of God, so that they might experience it lovingly in him, with him, and through him!

Ideally, the wedding should take place during the celebration of Mass. Why? Because married life is a form of Christian life, which like all life lived in faith is an offering to God and for his glory. This offering is, so to speak, an "insertion" into the offering Jesus made of himself to the Father on the altar of the Cross. It is an offering into which we as Christians insert ourselves by participation in the sacrifice of the Mass, for every time it is celebrated, it makes present the one sacrifice of Christ. Thus, we see clearly that the proper and natural way to celebrate Christian marriage is by joining intimately in Christ's offering to the Father, made sacramentally present in the Eucharist by the action of the Holy Spirit.

THE CHRISTIAN FAMILY AND HOME CONSTITUTE A DOMESTIC CHURCH

When a family has been constituted through the sacrament of marriage and when the spouses share the conviction that they have entered the Christian state of "married," their home takes on a special religious meaning. Naturally, the newlyweds will arrange it in such a way that it will be for themselves and their children welcoming, safe, and friendly. Whatever helps to make human life pleasant and agreeable cannot be displeasing to God, who invites us to enjoy all things that are good and in accord with his will, in joy and thanksgiving to God for his gifts. Family life becomes and is kept pleasant not only through the important things but also through the many small gestures that are expressions of love, sensitivity, and generosity.

As already mentioned, marriage has not only a material and temporal aspect but also a spiritual thrust that is already realized in this earthly stage of our life and points, definitively, to our final destiny beyond death in eternal life. For this reason, Christian spouses serenely accept the responsibility to help each other grow as disciples of Christ and willingly cooperate with God so that their children, the gift and blessing of their union, might become true Christians. This state of affairs is not achieved automatically; proper means must be used so that the grace of the sacrament might bear abundant fruit.

What are these means?

Naturally, the house or apartment where a Catholic family lives ought to be *blessed* by a priest or deacon, in order to beg God's help for all those who live there.

And certainly, the *Word of God*. The reading of Sacred Scripture and especially the Gospels, the *Catechism of the Catholic Church* and its *Compendium*, the lives of the saints and other writings that tell of God's saving plan and provide examples to encourage and strengthen the family on their journey.

Finally, *prayer*. Christian spouses should begin the day by lifting their hearts to God; it is good if the two of them can do this together, by offering the new day with its work, joys, and concerns and asking for his help and protection. Parents should teach their children to pray and pray with them. It is a beautiful practice to pray the Rosary every day as a family, recalling the mysteries of our Catholic faith and asking the protection of the Blessed Virgin Mary!

On *Sunday* and even on other days, if possible, the spouses should take part in the celebration of Mass, accompanied by their children, in order to renew the offering of their lives to the glory of God, and unite their offering to that which Christ made to the Father.

In a Catholic home there ought to be *sacred images* that will help maintain belief in God who is "in heaven, on earth, and in every place." Images of our Lord Jesus Christ and the Blessed Virgin Mary, as well as images of one or more saints who are objects of special devotion, cannot be absent. If the house is spacious, one room could be used as a *prayer room*; if the house is small, it would be fitting to at least set aside a place for a sacred image and possibly also a Bible, where the whole family could gather, even briefly, to pray.

It is a good and commendable practice to have a holy water font in the home, in order to make the Sign of the Cross with holy water. It recalls our Baptism and the consecration of our life to God amid the responsibilities and in the place where divine providence has placed us.

Thus the family home can be considered a "little domestic Church," as the Second Vatican Council calls it.

SEPARATION, DIVORCE, NULLITY OF MARRIAGE

In any marriage, there can be moments of tension. They may have their origin in attitudes of one spouse or the other, but often responsibility lies with both. It is desirable for both spouses to contribute to overcoming these difficulties, working together patiently, humbly, and forgivingly, treasuring the love that led them to establish a family, the love promised before the altar of God for the needs of the children and the good of society and the Church, which has family stability as one of its foundations. No sacrifice should be considered too great when it is a question of saving the unity of a marriage. Praying fervently to God to touch hearts and dispel misunderstandings is a basic element for overcoming moments of crisis. Humbly admitting one's mistakes can smooth over many difficulties. Asking a friend with good judgment and sound principles to mediate may be a reasonable course that can produce good and positive results.

Sometimes, despite a couple's sincere efforts, a severe crisis cannot be overcome, and, unfortunately, one spouse may become convinced that a break is inevitable. The reasons for reaching such an extreme situation must not be petty, such as stubbornness based on pride or a lack of generosity in seeking solutions. A decision must be contemplated over a long period of time and be made only after listening to the advice of impartial people who can be recommended for their experience of married life.

For very serious reasons, it may be legitimate to conclude that the only solution humanly possible is *separation*, that is, the discontinuation of married life together. The justifications for separation include one spouse threatening the life of the other spouse, life together plagued by physical or moral violence, risk to the moral integrity of the children, and other similarly grave reasons. When one reaches this extreme, painful, and unavoidable decision to separate, one must rebuild a life alone and trust in God. The separated spouse must still maintain marital fidelity, even though the other party may be gravely at fault. A person who is separated cannot legitimately and morally attempt to establish another marriage bond; that would mean, according to the clear teaching of Jesus, a fall into the sin and situation of *adultery*: "Whoever divorces his wife and marries another commits adultery against her; and if she divorces her husband and marries another, she commits adultery" (Mk 10:11 f.). A person who is separated and not living with another is not prevented from approaching the Sacrament of Reconciliation and receiving absolution and is allowed to approach the Eucharist to receive the Body and Blood of Christ.

In many countries, civil law has introduced *divorce*. This institution purports to break a validly established marriage bond and leave the people who have contracted it free to establish civilly a new family. If the people who divorce were united not only civilly but also sacramentally, the civil divorce has no effect on the church marriage, and the divorced person continues to be married before God. If a person has divorced solely for the property consequences, which cannot be otherwise obtained, and does not attempt to marry again civilly, that person can receive the sacraments of the Church, because he or she is not living in sin. But if that person marries again civilly, being already united in a true marriage before the Church, he or she ends up in a situation of *adultery* and cannot receive absolution from sin, much less Holy Communion, while remaining in that state.

There is another situation that may seem similar to divorce but is not: a *declaration of nullity of the marriage* issued by a tribunal of the Church. A *declaration of nullity* proves that what was *apparently* a marriage in reality *never was*, because there was a defect in the beginning that prevented its validity. While *divorce* purports to break and destroy a marriage bond recognized as valid and existing, a declaration of nullity is limited to recognizing that what was apparently a marriage in reality was not. To determine whether a marriage is null requires knowledge of canon law. What are the defects that can provide a basis for a declaration of nullity of a marriage? The subject is complicated, but here are a few examples of defects: having contracted marriage under severe pressure, that is, without the necessary freedom; having contracted marriage with a lack of maturity serious enough to prevent true consent to the marriage; being married to a person who was not free to marry because he or she was validly united in marriage to another person; being married to a person who is a very close blood relative; being incapable of carrying out the sexual relationship that is proper to marriage; being mistaken about the identity of the person one wished to marry. Again, a declaration of nullity means recognizing that something appeared to be a marriage but in reality never was. It is, *absolutely* distinct from divorce and separation. A declaration of nullity does not break a truly existing bond but declares that it was only *apparent* and did not correspond to the reality.

The Church has no power to break the bond of a marriage that was validly contracted between two baptized people and consummated through sexual relations: "Therefore, what God has joined together, no human being must separate" (Mt 19:6, Mk 10:9).

CONCLUSION

A fitting way to end this booklet is to cite two very beautiful texts from Sacred Scripture that refer to marriage.

The first is taken from the book of Tobit in the Old Testament:

When Sarah's parents left the bedroom and closed the door behind them, Tobiah rose from bed and said to his wife, "My sister, come, let us pray and beg our Lord to grant us mercy and protection." She got up, and they started to pray and beg that they might be protected. He began with these words:

"Blessed are you, O God of our ancestors;
    blessed be your name forever and ever!
Let the heavens and all your creation bless you forever.
You made Adam, and you made his wife Eve
    to be his helper and support;
    and from these two the human race has come.
You said, 'It is not good for the man to be alone;
    let us make him a helper like himself.'
Now, not with lust,
    but with fidelity I take this kinswoman as my wife.

> Send down your mercy on me and on her,
> > and grant that we may grow old together.
> > Bless us with children."

They said together, "Amen, amen!" Then they went to bed for the night. (Tb 8:4-9)

The second is taken from the letter of Saint Paul to the Ephesians:

> Husbands, love your wives even as Christ loved the church and handed himself over for her to sanctify her, cleansing her by the bath of water with the word, that he might present to himself the church in splendor, without spot or wrinkle or any such thing, that she might be holy and without blemish. So [also] husbands should love their wives as their own bodies. He who loves his wife loves himself. For no one hates his own flesh but rather nourishes and cherishes it, even as Christ does the church, because we are members of his body.

"For this reason a man shall leave [his] father and [his] mother
> and be joined to his wife,

and the two shall become one flesh."

> This is a great mystery, but I speak in reference to Christ and the church. In any case, each one of you should love his wife as himself, and the wife should respect her husband. (Eph 5:25-33)

Just as the Eucharist is the greatest sacrament by reason of its *content*, since in it Jesus Christ is really, truly, and substantially present with his Body, Blood, soul, and divinity, so marriage is the greatest by reason of its *meaning*, since it is the image of the merciful and saving love of Christ, the bridegroom, for the Church, his bride.

Do you realize how great is the sacrament and mystery of marriage? If you are planning to get married, have you grown aware of the temporal and spiritual responsibilities you will take upon yourself, responsibilities to yourself, to your spouse, and to the children God will entrust to you? If you are married, do you thank God for having called you to the married state? Do you frequently call to mind the greatness and the temporal and spiritual responsibilities arising from your state? Do you see your spouse as a son or daughter of God whom you must help on his or her pilgrimage to him? Do you see your children as precious gifts you have received from him and for whom you must do everything possible to direct to him? Do you celebrate your wedding anniversary every year, recalling with gratitude God's call to serve him in this state and renewing your covenant of faithfulness and love? When there is a marriage in crisis near you, have you offered these spouses help and advice to overcome their problems? Have you prayed for them and their children?

All that and much more, with joy, gratitude, effort, and prayer, you will do for the Lord with the help of his grace.